BECOMING YOU

BECOMING YOU

A simple guide to setting goals and accomplishing great things

STEPHANIE RICHEY

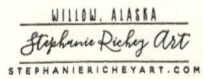

Stephanie Richey Art

Contents

1	Introduction	1
2	Where Am I Going	2
3	How Do I Get There	4
4	Priorities	7
5	Habits	12
6	Goals	17
7	Persevere	24
8	You Made It!	28
notes		29
About Me		31

Copyright © 2021 by Stephanie Richey

All rights reserved. No part of this book may be reproduced in any manner whatsoever without written permission except in the case of brief quotations embodied in critical articles and reviews.

First Printing, 2021

I

Introduction

This book is a series of blog posts from my website that I wanted to put together in a more comprehensive and complete form. It comes from my experiences with priorities, habits, setting goals and achieving them. This is only one of many ways I have found to help myself improve, and now hopefully to help someone else along in their path toward personal improvement. We are all unique in our learning and understanding, so this book may not help some, but I believe if you follow the steps, it will give you ideas on how to change and why it's important. You are worth the effort you put into making yourself the best you can be, and only you can create the changes you want to see. I hope you enjoy this book and that it can help you in the next steps of your life.

2

Where Am I Going

I don't think I have ever talked to a person who was 100% satisfied with who they were, every part of them. Not because they were not good people, but simply because they had the potential to be better, and they knew they did. We have an innate desire to do better, to be better, to strive for something more. It is human nature to do so, and that's a good thing! Imagine if we didn't, we would still live in the dark ages. No new technology, no new inventions, nothing ever changing.

Change, however, is hard. We get comfortable with where we are, even if we know we need to do better. Change often makes us uncomfortable because we can't see where we're going to end, maybe we don't know if what we are doing now will give us the desired results we want. But, however much we hate to admit it, change is happening to us all the time. But if we aren't the ones initiating it, then the change occurring is probably not the kind of change we are looking for.

I have thought a lot about this subject, as I want to be better, I want to do better in many aspects of my life. I am not a perfect person. But I have learned to embrace change, or at least most of the time. Over time

I have seen the fruits of change in my life. Some of that change came out of necessity, I didn't initiate it, but as time went on, I embraced it so that I would change how I wanted, instead of it changing me in ways that were detrimental to me or those around me. Most changes that I notice differences in however, I have initiated myself on some level or another. Goals I have set or habits I wanted to gain or get rid of. Some of these changes have been obvious to others, most are small changes in my character, that I wanted to make, or decided would be good for me, over a long period of time.

This book is designed to help you begin on a path that will hopefully never end. We should never stop growing, never stop learning, and never stop striving for excellence in our lives, because average is the enemy of excellence. Never settle for average, never settle for almost. You can become who you want to be, it just takes some work. This book will help you get started.

Think about your life. Are there things you are not satisfied with? Start here and list at least on general thing you would like to change. It doesn't have to be specific, and it can be as big or small as you want.

3

How Do I Get There

Often when we start noticing things in our lives that we aren't particularly proud of, or things we want to change, we wonder where to begin. We set goals, we look to the future, maybe we even write a few things down. As time passes, we lose interest in what we wanted to become. Sometimes it's because we think it's too hard, or we fall off the wagon and decide we'll never be able to get back on. Maybe the goal we set was too big for us, or maybe the steps getting there were so tall we couldn't even reach the next step on our tippy toes. Whatever the case may be, we need to stop. Our mind is the first thing we need to learn to control. Maybe there is some validity in some of those excuses, but they aren't a reason to quit, just a reason to reevaluate.

I love to exercise, and I like to be fit. There was a time in my life when I was exercising hard, at least sixty minutes a day, six days a week. I was a young mom, so I was chasing kids around all day, I was physically active all day long besides my workouts. I could tell that something was off, as I was not gaining energy any more from my workouts, I felt like I was slowly deteriorating, becoming more and more exhausted. But I wasn't losing weight, which was my goal. I was at the point of wanting to quit, because who wants to keep beating up their body for no results. But instead of quitting, I stopped; I reevaluated what I was doing. I prayed, because I do that a lot. I started to pay attention to what the fitness experts were saying. Eating healthy was a priority, but quantity of food was not something I had thought of. I set a goal to maintain a certain calorie count. I started to see results, measurable results. I didn't quit exercising; I adjusted the other part of my life that needed attention. I was able to reduce my exercise, and do it smarter when I ate more correctly. Then I got my energy back. So often different parts of our lives are interconnected, and when we work on one, we may have to visit a different area and work on two simultaneously. Sometimes getting one area of our lives in order will propel another area forward without even trying. Sometimes we realize we were focused on the wrong thing all along.

I hope that as you work through this book, you can identify areas of your life that need work, different areas that can maybe be done together, and which ones are the most important. After all, we only have so much time in a day. Making sure we start with what's most important and then working our way down the line will help us manage a smaller list, but get things in the correct order to begin with. That way we aren't working on the pennies all the time when we should be focusing on the dollars. Remember also, we are all a work in progress, once one goal becomes a habit, we can move on to the next. We don't have to do everything all at once, because we have a lifetime to get better.

We all have reasons we stop working toward goals and change. We rationalize quitting. These really only equate to rational lies that we use to convince ourselves we don't need to go on. But seeing them for what they are will help us avoid using them in the first place. Write them down on the next page so you can avoid them.

4

Priorities

Many years ago, I was sitting in a class about priorities. The teacher encouraged us to sit down when we got home and write down what our priorities were, and then rank them starting with the most important. I knew what my priorities were, but I decided to take this teacher's advice. Looking back, I really did know what my priorities were, but not the order that I wanted them to be in. This one simple activity has influenced how I make decisions and why, ever since then. It has also made larger decisions a lot simpler as I look at how it will affect those things that are most important to me.

Our priorities should govern the choices that we make. We can set new priorities as we progress, or as our lives change, but there are some, at least for me, that will never change, and they happen to be at the top of my list. When we have good priorities, it helps us to set better goals, better boundaries for our time and energy, and to achieve more conscientiously in our lives. As I talked about before, I love to exercise and eat healthy. When people ask me how I do it, I start talking about exercising and eating right. They quickly stop me and say, "you must just be blessed to look like that." Actually, no. It is a priority in my life to be healthy, and so I take the steps to be so. Sometimes we have a priority and then set a goal to maintain that, and then feel we have been restricted in some way. Sometimes we feel we are being inconvenienced suddenly, or punished because we now have this goal or priority that requires change. Priorities, and the goals associated with them are not punishment, but rather a means to an end, an end that at some point we felt like would be a good thing.

I am a religious person, and I strive to be obedient to the commandments that God has set for us. How often though, do people feel that the commandments are restrictions, that they are a good set of rules for everyone else, but we should be able to pick and choose. Commandments are not restrictions however; they are the guardrail that is keeping us on the road. Our priorities should be the same kind of thing. We have a destination we want to ultimately reach, and there is a road we need to take to get there. If we detour, we won't get there. If we swerve off the edge of the road or run through the guardrail, we won't get there. We need to remember why we set up that guardrail in the first place.

I will share with you several of my priorities and where they fall in my ordered list. Your list will look different than mine does, but I want you to really think about what is important to you, what order those things go in, and why they are on the list.

1 – My relationship with my Heavenly Father. This is the most important thing in my life. I want to return to live with Him, and the responsibility to do so lies solely with me. What do I do to make Him a priority? I read my scriptures every day. I pray many times a day, I learn about my Savior and try to emulate Him.

2 – My family. My husband first and then my kids. I also believe I can be with my family for eternity, and that starts with my husband. What do I do to make him a priority? When he needs help on a job, I

try to make time to go help him, I ride along to look at jobs, I go with him to get materials, and we go on a date almost every week. Sometimes the date is doing one of those things. What do I do to make my kids a priority? The things my kids want to learn, we explore. My daughter played basketball through high school. We went to games, I worked in the concessions stands to help the team, we set aside money for gear, hotels and food. When my kids were in elementary school, I spent a lot of hours volunteering, helping out in classes and on field trips. When they picked a high school that was twice as far away as the one in our area because of the opportunities, we did it. And most of all, when we were driving all those places, we talked. I am so grateful for the open relationship we have developed so that we can talk about anything.

3 – Being healthy. We all have genetic predisposition to things. Those things might even kill us in the end. But I always tell my kids, I want my genetics to kill me, not the fact that I wrecked my body because I didn't take care of myself. I want to postpone any genetic problems I might have for as long as possible. What do I do about it? I exercise 6 days a week and I strive to make healthy choices in what I take into my body. I try to get outside as often as possible, to be outside in the fresh air. These things have always had a positive impact on my life.

4 – My Church. Going to church is important to me, it makes my week go better. In my church we also have jobs or responsibilities to fulfill, and getting mine done is important to me. What do I do? This one is pretty simple, I go to church. I do my job, whatever that requires, and whatever days it is required (Some jobs happen on different days than Sunday.)

Everything else comes after these 4 priorities. Since I sat down and figured out the order, I have had so many times when good activities conflicted, or decisions were hard as they both seemed good, but when I really looked at what was important, it wasn't hard at all. For example, when one of my children had an event on the same night as a church activity, the child came first. When I have to choose between exercising today, or driving to Anchorage with my husband, not knowing if I'll have time later to get my workout in, I will go to town with my husband. Not because I don't want to exercise, but he is more important. He has shown that I am important to him as well though, by being willing to wait for me to finish my workout before we left.

Now it's your turn. Think about what is really important in your life. I would recommend thinking of more than one priority, but it doesn't have to be an extensive list as you can see from mine. But you can get as detailed as you'd like to be. Write these down in order of importance and then put your list somewhere you can see it for a while. You may decide things need to be shuffled. Once you have them pretty well how you want them, put them where you can find them, and when there is a decision to make, see where that decision falls in your list. Then move forward accordingly. And never apologize for your priorities. Other people may not understand, especially if they want you to do something for them, but they aren't living your life. You are.

Make a list of your priorities here, and give at least one reason why it is on your list. Put your list in order of importance, most important being at the top.

5

Habits

Habits are things we do all the time. Sometimes they can be unconscious things we do, like twirling a piece of hair when we talk, chewing our fingernails, how we brush our hair every day, and so on. Other habits are formed with more thought and considerations. Maybe we read or listen to the news from the same source, eat our meals at the same time every day, go the same route to work or the store, etc. Some habits are easy to develop, often without us even thinking about it, it's just how we've always done it. Others take more thought, more time, and often more effort.

We just finished talking about priorities, and what we find most important. I hope you wrote yours down so that you can refer to them often. Now we will look at habits how habits help us achieve those priorities or deter us from getting where we want to go. One thing to keep in mind is that getting rid of bad habits takes time and effort. We're not going to be perfect right at the beginning, so give yourself a little bit of leeway to make mistakes, learn from them, adjust if needed, and then keep moving forward. Give others the same opportunity to grow and change. I will relate a couple of instances from my own life to illustrate some of what I mean.

First, a really basic thing that all human's have to learn. The dreaded potty training. I remember when I was getting ready to potty train my oldest child, I read a number of articles about how to potty train, and they were all different, but one thing that was a common thread among a number of the articles was habits. They reminded me that my child had developed a habit of using the diaper and then being changed. It wasn't a bad habit; it's how things are in the beginning. Now I was going to try and change that habit so they would use the toilet instead. So, we were trying to break a bad habit and start a new habit. The point of all that was to give kids a little room to make mistakes. They weren't going to get it on the first day, and there was no reason to be angry when they made mistakes. How hard is it for an adult to break a bad habit, and we're trying to get a 2 year old to break one and start a new one all at the same time. I am so grateful for that advice as it changed my perspective and allowed me to be patient with the process. Patience with yourself and with others as they learn is vital.

The second is about exercise. I know I talk about this a lot, but I have found many other aspects in my life that the lessons I have learned from exercise apply to. Many years ago, at the beginning of a new year, I set a goal that is familiar to many people at the start of a new year. I wanted to lose weight. I decided the best way to go about doing that was to exercise 5 days a week. I bought several workout videos. There were weights, steps, a weighted bar, etc. Those workouts started hard, but as I kept at it, I actually started to enjoy working out. Fast forward to now, and that one goal, that one thing I persevered in doing so long ago has become a habit, one that I really enjoy! Do I miss days periodically? Yes. Do I beat myself up about it? No. But I also don't allow myself to get out of the habit. I make sure if I miss a day, it's only one. Now, with the streaming options online, even when I'm out of town I can find some way to exercise. It's just a matter of being determined to do it.

These stories illustrate an important lesson I think we all need to learn. Be patient, and don't give up. Habits don't form overnight, and bad habits aren't broken in a day. I hope you have started to think about habits you have, bad ones you might want to get rid of. Maybe you have good habits that just aren't as prominent in your life as you would like them to be. Maybe you have new ones you would like to incorporate into your life.

A few more lessons I have learned about habits. I learned that if I want something bad enough, I will work for it. I think sometimes we set a goal that seems nice, that other people are setting and looks fun, or that maybe we know would be good for us but our hearts really aren't in it. So, we need to make sure those goals, those habits we want to develop are appropriate for us personally. That we have thought through the steps we need to take to accomplish them. Good goals stretch us, and good habits are great ways to be stretched, but they still need to be accomplishable. Also remember that every goal hits a wall at some point. Everything that is important to us will be hard somewhere in the process, but that doesn't make it less worthwhile, that doesn't mean it shouldn't be accomplished or that we can't do it. It just means we have to press forward, even when we don't want to, even when we might not see the next step ahead or it feels like we are stepping out into the dark. Because the end result will be so much better than where we started.

Through my exercise I have learned that no matter what we do, we need to increase in some sort of strength. Whether it be stronger muscles, reading better, painting better, excelling at work, being a better parent. No matter the goal, it requires some sort of increase in mental, physical, or spiritual strength, and often all three. I have learned that by breaking down my muscles I am actually building them up. When we set goals, we need to remember that at some point it's going to be hard. We're breaking down who we were, and becoming something better. Don't give up just because it's hard.

I have also learned that sometimes we need cue's to help us remember. I love to read my scriptures, it falls into my priority list under number one, my relationship with my Heavenly Father. But how often I used to forget. I decided to coincide my spiritual feast with feeding my body. I now read my scriptures when I eat my breakfast, most of the time. This gave me a physical reminder of a spiritual goal that was super important to me. Now, even when we are not at home for breakfast, I still remember to read my scriptures because it is morning, and even if I didn't get a great breakfast, I can get some spiritual strength even when I'm not home. It has become a habit.

How do we develop these good habits? Remember your priority list? Make sure that the habit(s) you decide on first coincide with those priorities. If they do, you will be more motivated to accomplish your goals that will eventually turn into habits. Make time for them. If there is a habit we want to break, give less time to it. Some habits may need professional help, don't be afraid of getting the help you need to achieve what you want to achieve. There is no shame in bettering yourself. Don't listen to people who try to discourage you from positive changes you are trying to make. There will be a lot of critics. Ignore them.

Now that we've discussed habits, take some time to write down at least one thing you would like to change, get rid of, or start doing. Habits you would like to develop or others you would like to break. If you have a bad habit you are trying to break, it is often beneficial to have a good habit you want to develop as this will take the place of the time you were using in the old habit. Some suggestions – reducing your time on social media, video games or electronic devices as a whole by using your time on your devices for reading, exercising, or learning a new skill like baking or painting, etc. Another idea is to pair your habit with something you already do, like I did with my scripture reading. Write these down, and in the next section we will talk about goals.

What habit(s) do you want to start, or break? Write them down here and list which priority they fall under. If it's one you want to break, write down why. The why's can be motivational in our pursuit to change.

_____

_____

_____

_____

_____

_____

_____

_____

_____

_____

_____

_____

_____

6

Goals

We have now talked about priorities, and how they affect our decision making. We just finished talking about habits, and some ways to develop and/or get rid of different kinds of habits. But how do we develop habits? That is where goals come in. Some people hear the word goal and they are immediately done. They like to go through life deciding each day what they want to do, often on a whim. The problem with that is not having priorities, or a clear destination you are aiming toward. If you don't make a plan, you don't set out a road map for yourself, you really have no way of knowing how to get there. Often people who don't set goals find themselves in the same situations 20 year down the road. They haven't grown, changed, or gotten any better, and usually they, if not others around then, are worse off for it. We were not meant to float through life, but to achieve. To become excellent. Remember, average is the enemy of excellence. There are plenty of average people in this world, what we really need is excellence.

Goals come in many forms. We have big goals, small goals, dreams that could be goals, goals that have gone by the wayside for one reason or another. One of the problems with most goals is that we get started and we don't know how to continue, or it becomes a little more difficult than we thought and we decided that maybe that wasn't what we wanted after all. But just like our muscles, our goals should make us work, sometimes just a little bit, others may make us stretch beyond our comfort zone. That's a good thing.

I have rarely been a New Years Resolutions kind of person. I have done that in the past, but the drive to complete those goals hasn't always been there, consequently they have fallen by the way side. Sometimes that's not a bad thing, priorities change, but sometimes I would be so much further ahead or better off if I had just stuck with it a little bit longer. As I have gone along though, I have learned that there is never a bad time to set goals. Consequently, when the new year rolls around, I already have things I am working on now and have no desire to set a new year's resolution just because everyone else is.

How do we set goals? Setting effective goals is vital to our progression, so how do we go about doing that? I would encourage you to look back at what we have talked about already. You may already have some goals in mind, because most of what we strive for has to do with priorities and habits in our lives. I play the piano. I love playing the piano. But it is not always easy finding the time to do so. But as I think about why I play; I am reminded of my priorities. How does piano fit into my 4 priorities? Health. There is so much to do with brain function, dexterity, and eye/hand coordination and spatial awareness. These are all good for a healthy brain. But when I forget to practice, especially the older I get, I find that I have to really practice a lot to get back to where I was. Consequently, I set a goal to practice 4 days a week, 30 minutes each time. This is a bare minimum just to maintain. I have also set a goal to be willing to play the piano for others whenever a need arises. Whether it be in church, a funeral, a Christmas concert, etc. These are great as its new music and I have to practice a lot more to make sure I can play the songs well. It is also incentive to practice because I wouldn't want to have to tell someone no because my ability was diminishing. I have also told many people I am willing, so there is an accountability to others.

Now, look at your priority list, your list of habits as well, and decide on a goal. It doesn't matter how big it is, sometimes it helps to start off small. Think about how it relates to your priorities and your habits. Some may not have anything to do with either and may just be something you would like to do. But if it's important to you, it should be on your priority list somewhere. If it's not there, add it so that you will be more inclined to do it. Post your goal where you can see it every day. It needs to be in the front of your mind. This next step can be hard, but tell someone you know you can trust to support you. It may be the world through social media, it may be a personal confidant. But tell someone you know will check on you in an appropriate way, a helpful way. This will hold you accountable.

As I have exercised over the years I have learned that goals need to be measurable. Just like on a road there are mile markers, you need mile markers on your big goals that you can look at along the way. I love to exercise, but the only tool of measurement I used to use was the scale. If your goal is to be more fit, don't use the scale as your only tool of measure, it doesn't give you enough information. I like to remember, the only thing the scale can tell you by itself is how much gravitational pull the earth has on your body. Likewise, your goals need more than a generic marker that has little relevance. As I learned about fitness, I learned about body fat as compared to lean body mass, I learned how to use the scale as a tool. Tape measures, or body fat calipers are great tools that work with the scale to give you more information. If you are only using the scale, it can be very discouraging to see little or no change, or even a weight increase. It can make you want to quit. But using the other tool as well will help you know that often what really happens is that you have swapped muscle for fat, and you are leaner than you were even if you don't weigh any less. That is a step in the right direction and can motivate you to continue.

The next step then, is to break your goals up into measurable segments. Back to the fitness goal above, maybe instead of a change in the number on the scale, it could be an inch less body mass total, if you are measuring with a tape measure, or a decrease in your body fat percent measured by a fat caliper. Write down those steps, those mile markers so you know what your next step is. Don't set it too high. If you have 20 pounds to lose it'll take about 3 months to lose it. I know to some people that seems like forever, but in that time, if you are consistent, you will develop some really good habits that can propel you forward to complete that goal and start a new one. If you hit a plateau in your goals, which will happen, reevaluate. If it's fitness, look at what you've been eating, how much you've been exercising, adjust as you go along. It's ok to change the small goals when needed to get to the bigger goal. If you have plateaued out with any goal, figure out why. I recently set a painting goal which I have put on hold. I am taking an online watercolor course, but I hit a plateau and almost decided to unsubscribe to the lessons. However, in stopping to think about it, I realize that maybe what I needed was a break from the course and an opportunity to paint some of the other things I wanted to, for myself and others. I have found a renewed excitement for painting by doing so, and look forward now to continuing to learn from my class when I finish the painting I am working on. One reason is that in applying what I learned from the class I can see that my painting ability and knowledge of how to control the paints has increased because of the class, and I want to learn more. Adjust when needed, but never give up.

Remember that an important step in setting any goal is to celebrate the small victories as well as the big ones. Every time you reach the next step be proud of yourself. Sometimes a reward associated with each step is helpful. Rewards don't have to be physical. If you have found the right person to talk to about your goal, their excitement at your progress can be enough to help you keep moving forward. Once you have accomplished your original goal, don't stop. My first fitness goal was to complete one set of workout videos. If I had stopped there, I would never have developed a habit. My fitness goals now revolve around completing different programs at different times of the year, as well as testing my fitness level out in the real world through hiking, running, biking, etc. There is always something ahead to strive for. Keep looking forward, and only look back to see areas of improvement, and especially to see the progress you've made. That progress you see will help you move ahead with current and future goals.

The last thing I think might be the most important part of goal setting. That is to visualize yourself where you want to be. When you review your goals daily, see yourself accomplishing them. See yourself at the finish line. When my kids have learned to play basketball, especially to shoot foul shots, they have been told by countless coaches, you have to see the ball going in the hoop. When the kids can focus and allow themselves to do that, their foul shot percentages increase exponentially. See yourself where you want to be.

Take time now to write down at least one goal on the next page. Tell someone what that goal is. Evaluate the steps you need to take to get there. Make sure those steps are manageable, and write them down below the big goal. Reevaluate often to make sure they are still manageable and heading you in the right direction. If not, look at your goal from a different perspective and readjust. Sometimes talking to someone else will give you ideas you may not have thought about. Celebrate the little victories along the way. See yourself accomplishing your goal, see yourself at the finish line. And then never quit. Even when one goal is finished set a new one, keep progressing.

Goal(s): _____

_____

_____

_____

_____

Who will I tell: _____

_____

Steps: _____

_____

_____

_____

_____

How will I measure progress: _____

_____

_____

_____

_____

What will I use as a visual reminder: _____

_____

_____

_____

_____

Rewards (these can be very motivating): _____

_____

_____

_____

_____

Start date: _____

Completion date: _____

7

Persevere

The last thing to talk about here is perseverance. We can set all the goals in the world, want to develop all the great habits, and have the greatest intentions, but if we don't persevere through the difficulties involved, we will never make it to the end. We all have a choice every day to give up or keep going. No one is perfect, especially me, but every day I can get up and show up, striving to do my best, or I can give up. I remember really early on in developing my website, I was trying to get the program to do something, and it wasn't working. Nothing I did seemed to be working anymore. I was extremely frustrated with the computer, but even more so with myself and my apparent lack of ability to learn. I stood up from my computer, everyone else was in the room watching a movie, and very frustrated said how stupid I was, and I couldn't learn anything! I left the room very discouraged and went to my room to cool down. I'm sure my family was stunned. I don't usually let my frustrations out in such a vocal manner. As I cooled down, and asked my Heavenly Father if I truly was stupid, I had an overwhelming feeling of peace, and a thought to try again tomorrow. The next day I resumed my efforts with my website, and found that overnight everything I had tried to do had worked, it had just taken time for those changes to take effect. That lesson has helped me as I continue to modify and work on my website, as some things seem to be instantaneous, while others take several hours to work correctly. I am grateful I was instructed to have patience, grateful for the ability to have that patience, and grateful I didn't scrap the whole project that night.

Perseverance to me is the difference between our initial goals and success. Dreams are great to have, goals are great to set, but it is by daily choosing to take the steps necessary that we accomplish those goals, that those dreams become a reality. No matter what our goals are we will hit a wall. Perseverance means to figure out how to get through, over, under, or around that wall. More and more today I see people afraid to fail. Everything needs to be perfect; everything needs to be laid out ahead of time so that there is no guessing. Often my husband or I will send our kids on an errand or have a task for them to complete. They used to ask a lot of questions, how to do this or that, they spent so much time asking questions that they could have been done by the time they were finished asking questions. Often, if we chose to answer the questions, they couldn't comprehend the answers because they hadn't completed any of the steps in the process to even understand what we were talking about. We now give them basic instruction and tell them to figure it out. If for some reason they reach a stopping point where they really can't proceed, then come and ask. And if they don't do it exactly how we thought, we've also learned, there is more than one right way to do just about anything. Allowing them to figure it out and be successful helps them know they can do hard things, and persevere through other areas of their lives when things get hard.

When Thomas Edison was inventing the lightbulb, it took upwards of 10,000 attempts before he got it right. He was asked how it felt to fail so many times. His reply was that he had not failed 10,000 times, he had successfully discovered 10,000 ways which did not work. Failure is a perception. How often do we hit that wall and then think we failed? It can be very discouraging if we have the wrong mindset. But failure only happens when we give up. If we continue trying, then an unsuccessful attempt is simply data that can be applied to the next attempt. When we organize that data we can proceed forward, either in the same direction, making minor adjustments, or completely change course, whatever is needed to reach that ultimate goal. But if our goal is something we really want, we need to persevere through the data so that we can arrive at the end goal.

We are born with an innate ability to persevere through difficulties. If I fell down as many times as a toddler learning to walk, I think I might give up on walking. No matter what a small child does, they persevere through difficulties and they learn. They are fun to watch, and can be an inspiration to us as we think about our own challenges, trials or goals, and how to work through them. I am grateful for how the Lord has set up the earth and time. We have about 16 hours in a day to work on things, and then we get to sleep. What's awesome is that we get to wake up and start again. It's a new day, a new beginning, every day. Even if we didn't do as good, or complete as many tasks as we hoped, we can begin again in the morning, often with a fresh perspective and renewed energy to move forward.

Perseverance through life requires us to know what we want and where we are going. That's the priorities, and goal setting from earlier. If we don't know these two things, then it really doesn't matter what we do. I love the famous Cheshire cat quote from Alice in Wonderland: "If you don't know where you are going any road will get you there." Without our dreams and goals, we won't know where we are going, and instead of persevering to an end we chose, we end up just floating along, being taken wherever the current flows. The problem with that end is it's usually not where we expected or wanted to be. I can't find the author to the last quote, but this is one that I love, and hear often in my workout videos. It's inspirational to me to keep going, to keep moving forward regardless of how well I did the day before, to persevere through everything life throws at me, and to put in the effort for what is really important to me. It says: "Don't be upset by the results you didn't get with the work you didn't do." Author Unknown

I would encourage you to decide on some things you might do to help you keep going when it gets hard. Quotes often help me, and you can find them in my kitchen, my bedroom, on my phone etc. Pictures help people make better choices; some people find a motivational collage of pictures to be helpful. I encourage you to find something that will help you keep going, help you visualize success, because your success is worth the work.

What motivates me: _____

_____

_____

_____

How will I push through my walls: _____

_____

_____

_____

_____

Create something today that will inspire you to keep going when you plateau. Something that will help you push through that plateau to complete your goal.

8

You Made It!

Ok, so maybe it wasn't your goal to finish this book, but if you worked through it and wrote some things down, you now have a plan to do great things in the future, starting today!

You are worth the effort that you put into yourself. You can accomplish great things over time, but you can't accomplish anything if you don't start. I hope you start today on a life long journey of change and progress.

As you progress along, remember that we become better as we help others become better. Encourage those around you, be that good friend that will be kind when someone else is trying to change and do better. When we lift others, we find ourselves lifted as well.

Always remember to be kind to yourself along the way. You are doing a great work that will take time, but it is so worth the effort. You are so worth the effort.

About Me

Hi, my name is Stephanie Richey. I live in Alaska. I am an artist, writer, piano player, and I love the outdoors. I am also a wife and a mom. A lot of my time has been spent raising kids and helping my husband with his business until the last few years when I have had a little more time to do some things I wanted to do. I've always played the piano and did a lot of sewing through the years, but in the last 5 or so years I have also learned to paint, learned to make a website, and learned a lot about products. I have been sharing my thoughts on my blog and recently saw a theme, and so I took a chance at writing a book. This has been a new learning process, but learning something new is a great thing. If you enjoyed my book, you can read more of my blog posts as well as see my art on my website at: stephaniericheyart.com

www.ingramcontent.com/pod-product-compliance
Lightning Source LLC
LaVergne TN
LVHW090054080526
838200LV00082B/3